FACT CAT

FISH

Izzi Howell

WAYLAND
www.waylandbooks.co.uk

FACT CAT

Get your paws on this fantastic new mega-series from Wayland!

Join our Fact Cat on a journey of fun learning about every subject under the sun!

First published in Great Britain in 2015 by Wayland

Copyright © Wayland 2015

All rights reserved

ISBN: 978 0 7502 9600 7

Dewey Number: 597-dc23

10 9 8 7 6 5 4 3 2 1

MIX
Paper from responsible sources
FSC® C104740

Wayland

An imprint of Hachette Children's Group

Part of Hodder & Stoughton

Carmelite House

50 Victoria Embankment

London EC4Y 0DZ

An Hachette UK Company

www.hachette.co.uk

www.hachettechildrens.co.uk

A catalogue for this title is available from the British Library

Printed and bound in China

Produced for Wayland by White-Thomson Publishing Ltd
www.wtpub.co.uk

Editor: Izzi Howell

Design: Clare Nicholas

Fact Cat illustrations: Shutterstock/Julien Troneur

Other illustrations: Stefan Chabluk

Consultant: Kate Ruttle

Picture and illustration credits:

Corbis: David Shale/Nature Picture Library 21; iStock: qldian title page, tingfen 4tl, qldian 4bl, viridis 5, strmko 6, ifish 9, renacali 17, Whitepointer 18; Shutterstock: iliuta goean cover, frantisekhojdysz 4tr, Songsak Pandet 4br, Mirko Rosenau 7t, Hayati Kayhan 7b, LauraD 8, Filip Fuxa 10t, stockpix4u 10b, Richard Whitcombe 11, Rich Carey 12, Amanda Nicholls 13, Levent Konuk 14, Rich Carey 15 and 16, Peter Leahy 19, Beth Swanson 20.

The author, Izzi Howell, is a writer and editor specialising in children's educational publishing.

The consultant, Kate Ruttle, is a literacy expert and SENCO, and teaches in Suffolk.

FACT CAT FACT

There is a question for you to answer on each spread in this book. You can check your answers on page 24.

CONTENTS

WHAT IS A FISH?

Fish are a group of animals that are similar to each other in certain ways. Fish live underwater and breathe using **gills**. Most fish are covered in **scales**.

Leafy sea dragons, hammerhead sharks, eagle rays and koi carp are all types of fish.

leafy sea dragon

hammerhead shark

eagle ray

koi carp

Almost all fish are **cold-blooded**. Cold-blooded animals can't control the temperature of their bodies. They have a high temperature in warm water, and a low temperature in cold water.

Butterflyfish need to stay warm to **survive** so they live in **tropical** seas and oceans.

FACT CAT FACT

Although jellyfish and starfish have the word 'fish' in their name, they are not fish. This is because fish have **backbones**, but jellyfish and starfish do not. Can you find out another animal with 'fish' in its name that isn't a fish?

HABITAT

Some fish live in the **salt water** of seas and oceans. Many of the fish that we eat, such as cod and mackerel, come from **temperate** and **polar** oceans.

FACT CAT FACT

Bull sharks and river sharks can live in both salt water and fresh water. In South America, bull sharks have been found in rivers that are thousands of kilometres from the sea!

Most sharks, such as this grey reef shark, live in salt water.

Many fish live in **freshwater** lakes and rivers. Some freshwater fish are very large, such as the 180-kilogram arapaima. Others are small, such as neon tetras, which are only 3 centimetres long.

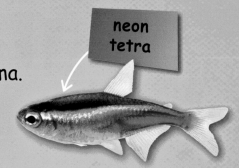

neon tetra

Shoals of red-bellied piranhas swim together in the lakes and rivers of South America. What do red-bellied piranhas eat?

BREATHING

Like all animals, fish need **oxygen** to survive. Instead of getting oxygen from the air as humans do, almost all fish get oxygen from water.

Fish, such as this lionfish, swallow water so that they can take oxygen from it.

As water passes through a fish's body, its gills take oxygen from the water. Then, the fish's gills open to let the water flow out of its body.

A fish's gills are on the side of its head.

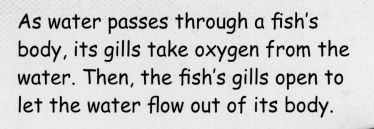

gills

FACT CAT FACT

The lungfish takes in oxygen from the air as well as from water. Lungfish can leave the water and live on land in mud **burrows**. Can you find out another fish that can live out of water?

SKIN

Fish have different kinds of scales. Most fish are covered in large, smooth scales, but sharks and rays have small, hard scales.

Goldfish have smooth scales that lie on top of each other. This makes it easier for them to swim through the water.

Shark skin is so rough that other animals can get hurt if they touch it.

The colour of a fish's scales can help it to hide from **predators**. Fish that live far from the **coast** are often blue or black so that they match the colour of the deep water.

The longnose hawkfish has a striped pattern which looks like the **coral reef** where it lives.

FACT CAT FACT

The cleaner wrasse fish cleans the skin of other fish! How does it do this?

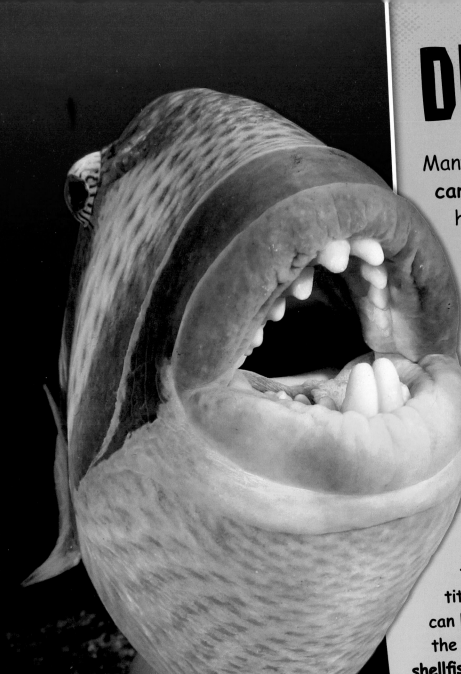

DIET

Many fish are **carnivores**. They have sharp teeth that help them to catch and eat other animals for food.

The strong teeth of this titan triggerfish can break through the hard shells of **shellfish**, such as crabs.

The whale shark only eats plankton. It uses the **filter** in its mouth to take plankton out of the water.

Many freshwater and saltwater fish eat **plankton**. Plankton are extremely small animals and plants that live in water. Fish that eat plankton are **omnivores**, because they eat both plants and animals.

FACT CAT FACT

Whale sharks are the largest fish on Earth. They are up to 12 metres long, which is longer than a bus! How much does a whale shark weigh?

YOUNG

Most fish **young** are born from eggs. **Female** fish lay their eggs in the water.

This clownfish has laid its eggs on the side of a rock.

eggs

FACT CAT FACT

The eggs of the sturgeon fish are one of the most expensive foods in the world. What is another name for this dish?

Some female fish leave their eggs to hatch on their own. Other fish stay with their eggs and take care of their young after they are born.

Many sharks give birth to live young. This whitetip reef shark was born ready to look after itself.

MOVEMENT

Most fish swim by moving their body and tail in an 's' shape. This movement pushes them forwards through the water.

This bigeye fish uses its **fins** to move up and down in the water.

Not all fish move in the same way. Rays move through the water by flapping their fins. Eels use the muscles in their long bodies to swim forwards, just as a snake moves across land.

Manta rays can jump out of the water for a few seconds.

SENSES

One of the most important senses for fish is sight. Most fish can see well from far away and recognise different colours.

This great white shark smells through holes in its nose called nostrils. Most sharks have an excellent sense of smell.

nostril

FACT CAT FACT

Great white sharks can smell blood in the water from 5km away! Are great white sharks **herbivores**, carnivores or omnivores?

lateral
line

The **lateral line** along the side of a fish's body can sense movement and sound in the water. This lets fish know if there is a predator nearby.

The lateral line of this Spanish hogfish starts from its eye and ends by its tail.

STRANGE FISH

When the pufferfish senses danger, it swallows a lot of water. The extra water in its body makes it grow much bigger, which means that predators won't want to eat it.

This pufferfish has spines on its skin that stick out when it puffs up.

FACT CAT FACT

If a predator eats a pufferfish, it is likely that the predator will die. Pufferfish are one of the most poisonous animals on Earth!

There isn't much light down in the deep ocean. Some deep ocean fish make their own light to bring **prey** towards them.

The female anglerfish has a light hanging off its head. How did the anglerfish get its name?

Try to answer the questions below. Look back through the book to help you. Check your answers on page 24.

1 Starfish are fish. True or not true?

a) true

b) not true

2 Where do red-bellied piranhas live?

a) Africa

b) Europe

c) South America

3 Almost all fish get oxygen from water. True or not true?

a) true

b) not true

4 What do carnivores eat?

a) plants

b) other animals

c) plants and other animals

5 Female fish lay their eggs out of the water. True or not true?

a) true

b) not true

6 Which of these fish is poisonous?

a) pufferfish

b) anglerfish

c) clownfish

GLOSSARY

backbone the line of bones down the centre of the back

burrow a hole that an animal digs in the ground to live in

carnivore an animal that only eats meat

coast the area of land that is next to the ocean

cold-blooded describes an animal whose body temperature depends on the temperature of their surroundings

coral reef a tropical sea habitat made from coral

female describes fish that can give birth to live young or lay eggs, from which young will hatch

filter something that you use to take a solid out of a liquid

fin a thin triangular part of a fish's body that is used to help them move through water

freshwater water that does not contain salt and is found in lakes or rivers

gill a part of the body that fish breathe through

herbivore an animal that only eats plants

lateral line a line along the side of a fish's body that helps it to sense movement

live describes something that is alive

omnivore an animal that eats plants and meat

oxygen a gas in the air that animals need to breathe to live

plankton very small plants and animals that live in the ocean and are eaten by other animals

polar describes an ocean with cold water

predator an animal that kills and eats other animals

prey an animal that is killed and eaten by other animals

salt water water that contains salt and is found in the sea or ocean

scales small pieces of hard skin that cover the bodies of fish

shellfish sea animals that have a hard outer shell for a body

shoal a large group of fish that swim together

survive to stay alive and not die

temperate describes an ocean with some warm and some cold water

tropical describes an ocean with warm water

young an animal's babies

INDEX

ANSWERS

Pages 4–21

Page 5: Some examples include shellfish and cuttlefish.

Page 7: Fish, insects and plants

Page 9: Mudskippers and some eels

Page 11: By eating the dead skin of other fish.

Page 13: 18.7 tonnes

Page 14: Caviar

Page 17: Tuna, swordfish and other large fish

Page 18: Carnivores

Page 21: From the light that hangs off its head that looks like a fisherman (angler) with a fishing line.

Quiz answers

1   not true – they do not have backbones.

2   c - South America

3   true

4   b - other animals

5   not true – they lay their eggs in the water.

6   a - pufferfish

OTHER TITLES IN THE FACT CAT SERIES...

Space
The Earth 978 0 7502 8220 8
The Moon 978 0 7502 8221 5
The Planets 978 0 7502 8222 2
The Sun 978 0 7502 8223 9

United Kingdom
England 978 0 7502 8927 6
Northern Ireland 978 0 7502 8942 9
Scotland 978 0 7502 8928 3
Wales 978 0 7502 8943 6

Countries
Brazil 978 0 7502 8213 0
France 978 0 7502 8212 3
Ghana 978 0 7502 8215 4
Italy 978 0 7502 8214 7

History
Neil Armstrong 978 0 7502 9040 1
Amelia Earhart 978 0 7502 9034 0
Christopher Columbus 978 0 7502 9031 9
The Wright Brothers 978 0 7502 9037 1

Habitats
Ocean 978 0 7502 8218 5
Rainforest 978 0 7502 8219 2
Seashore 978 0 7502 8216 1
Woodland 978 0 7502 8217 8

Geography
Continents 978 0 7502 9025 8
The Equator 978 0 7502 9019 7
The Poles 978 0 7502 9022 7
Seas and Oceans 978 0 7502 9028 9

Early Britons
Anglo-Saxons 978 0 7502 9579 6
Roman Britain 978 0 7502 9582 6
Stone Age to Iron Age 978 0 7502 9580 2
Vikings 978 0 7502 9581 9

WAYLAND
www.waylandbooks.co.uk